EVALUATING YOUR EXECUTIVE

New Approaches, New Purposes

Donn F. Vickers

Kelly Stevelt Kaser

Table of Contents

Section Three: Then Comes Action

Foreword

You are right. It will take time and thought to do this evaluation with your executive. You will have to make space in an already full organizational schedule where little space seems to exist. But in terms of importance and impact the executive evaluation experience ranks up there with keeping faith with the mission, making good strategic plans and securing the necessary resources to make it all work.

We presume to advocate for executive evaluation because we believe the various studies that show that two-thirds of our executive directors have no regular evaluation at all. We are emboldened to push on this because fewer than one-third of executive directors feel that their boards challenge them to be more effective (that from a 2006 CompassPoint study).

Think of it as a gift to your executive that like most good gifts benefits the giver and everyone else around as well. When evaluation is done with care and thoughtfulness your executive is encouraged in their professional development, the partnership between your board and your executive is strengthened and the organization becomes a more focused and reflective kind of place. Our hope is that this small volume will help you get all those benefits and more from your experience with executive evaluation.

In these pages our editorial committee has had the last word (see "Afterwords" on p. 51); they also had the first words with us as we initially sat down to think through what most needed to be said. Their own rich and varied experiences as board presidents and executives informed and inspired much of what is here and we are grateful to them for it.

We also feel fortunate to have a Board of Governors whose attitudes and insights are so hospitable to this kind of work. They are cherished colleagues and co-creators in all that we do.

Once again our efforts have been supported by Elfi DiBella and all the good people at the Huntington Bank. Their special brand of loyalty and generosity mean the world to us. Yet another example of dependable generosity is Dan Morris and Grange Insurance, who stepped in at the end to do the printing. And these pages are touched with an unusual combination of clarity and artistry because of our friend and editor Laura Bidwa who in fact, among many other things, is a fine artist.

Finally, our last and strongest appreciation is reserved for you board members who month by month do so much to shepherd and strengthen our not-for-profit organizations. It is to you that we dedicate this small book.

Donn F. Vickers
Kelly Stevelt Kaser
July 2006

Chapter I

A Place to Start

The State of the Art

It is not a difficult matter to collect criticism about executive evaluation. Perhaps the ultimate criticism is that it does not happen. Most estimates are that sixty to seventy-five percent of not-for-profit executives have no regular evaluation by the boards they serve. And, not uncommon is the report that a sizeable majority of those who do receive evaluations do not have a positive assessment of that experience.

This is not a not-for-profit CEO problem alone. Writing in the *Wall Street Journal*, Tim Schellhardt asks, "If less than ten percent of your customers judged a product effective and seven of ten said they were more confused than enlightened by it, you would drop it, right? So why don't companies drop their annual performance reviews?" Whether executive evaluation is administered to not-for-profit CEOs or for-profit CEOs, the questions are many and the criticisms severe:

> "Most performance review systems reinforce a paternalistic world, one built on distrust and the assumption that the boss (or board) knows more about our skills, abilities and commitments than we do. This dependency works against empowerment. And focusing on individual problems rather than looking at system issues works against the grain of quality improvement." —Rick Mauer

> "The basic nature of performance appraisals is [that] the board (or boss) takes responsibility for development...and exercises that responsibility through a discussion of strengths and weaknesses. This is an exercise of sovereignty regardless of how lovingly it is done. It makes no sense to talk of team- and partnership-oriented cultures...and still hold on to this artifact called performance appraisal." —Peter Block

> "It takes the average CEO six months to recuperate from the typical performance appraisal." —Tom Peters

So what to do? Well, what we hope to do in these pages is three things:

1. Encourage board members to regularly and thoughtfully evaluate their executive.

2. Enable your board to go about the tasks of evaluation in a way that promotes learning and strengthens the trust between board and executive.

3. Present a variety of evaluation inventories and processes, from which you may choose the ones that fit the culture of your organization.

What we will not do is assume that all of you on every board ought to go about this evaluation task in the same way. We greatly favor putting you and your fellow board members in charge of determining the "what works best for us" question. You can and should take hold of the distinctive culture and mission of your place and fashion the kind of evaluation processes that match who you are and what you value.

What You Can Find Elsewhere

Just so you know, we are aware of "360 evaluations" and we have chosen not to discuss them here. While they have gained popularity in recent years, it is our judgment that they are most helpful when conducted by a highly skilled consultant who can be sensitive to the nuances of expressions received from all the many statements that result, including both written responses and interviews. Herein, we have chosen to emphasize ways of evaluation that can be effectively carried out by thoughtful board members without the assistance of consultants.

We also know about the concept of so-called "stretch goals" that often shows up in materials on executive evaluation. We believe that in the not-for-profit world executives tend to be driven by a radical commitment to mission—therefore, not-for-profit boards usually have the task of encouraging sanity, not additional stretching. This puts us in line with the leadership philosophy of Scott Adams, the creator of the cartoon *Dilbert*, who in a recent strip has the boss saying, "Here are your stretch goals." Asked, "What's the difference?" the boss replies, "The regular goals can be achieved by sacrificing your health and your personal life… The stretch goals require all of that plus some sort of criminal conduct."

Finally, while we do understand that traditionally some evaluations have occurred at the same time as salary reviews and even determined the extent of compensation, we will not discuss evaluation in that context. Salaries should be reviewed with care on an annual basis and done so with attention to such matters as changes in the consumer price index, the size of the organizational budget and the regional norms for executive compensation in similar-sized organizations. Done well, the annual salary review is a big enough task in and of itself; that is why we include information and approaches for salary review in Chapter 4. The point here is that to mix a salary review with an evaluation experience aimed at reflective practice, professional development and strengthening the partnership between board and CEO is asking too much. When it is attempted, our experience is that the salary review is done without adequate research into financial criteria and the broader goals of the evaluation are pushed aside by the talk about money.

What You Will Find Here

What we promise to do is assist you as a board member to be more comfortable with the task of executive evaluation. We want you to see that it gets done and to understand that doing it can promote professional development for your executive and strengthen the relationship between you and the executive. Finally, we will offer you a range of evaluation inventories and processes from which to select the ones that best fit your organization.

All this we will do in the three broad sections that follow. In "First Comes Thought" we will help you think about the key issues involved in executive evaluation. We will suggest setting a tone that maximizes the likelihood that the evaluation experience will produce positive results for your board and your executive. We will also note some important conversations to have before beginning the actual evaluation. In "Now Comes Design" we will assist you in shaping an evaluation process that works for you, your organization and your executive. This section contains not only important evaluation details, but also a review of the purposes your own evaluation process can be designed to serve, including assistance with the issue of salary review. Finally, in "Then Comes Action," we will introduce you to fifteen evaluation processes from which you can choose, first in summary and then in detail. They range from traditional checklists with rating scales to lists of questions and quotations selected to initiate significant evaluation conversations.

In all that is here we urge you to select the parts and pieces that make sense for you and your situation. There is no one way that is best for all. The only thing we believe really is best for all is that executive evaluation happens and you experience all the benefits and satisfaction of doing it well.

Section One

First Comes Thought

Chapter 2

Setting a Tone and
Having a Conversation

We hope that you will put aside the temptation to jump ahead, select a tool and get on with it. So much in our organizations and the broader society pushes us to action and urges us to bypass reflection. Sometimes that is necessary and sometimes it works—but most of us have at one time or another experienced the unfortunate consequences of the ready, fire, aim school of organizational life.

There are, we believe, some important issues to be addressed before you move to the action step of the actual evaluation. There is the matter of setting the right tone for the evaluation experience. There are conversations about expectations that need to be had. And there are some additional considerations about the content of your evaluation, the message it will send and, not least of all, the special character of the not-for-profit culture that impacts the evaluation process.

Setting a Tone: Energizing, Not Enervating

This would be the wrong tone: A large boss sits behind a large desk in a large room in a recent *New Yorker* cartoon. Across the desk sits a small, somewhat bewildered-looking man and the boss says, "Do you mind if I give you a little destructive criticism?"

That scene both pictures and produces what "enervating" is all about and what you need to try to avoid: large over small, powerful over bewildered, negative aggression and passive reception. Words like "weaken," "exhaust" and "debilitate" come to mind. Who could think these are positive? Yet too many executives come away from their evaluation experience feeling just that way: less competent, less powerful, less confident and more confused about what is expected of them. Any one of those is not a good thing and taken together they are very much not a good thing.

What we know about ourselves is that when, for whatever reason, we are lacking in confidence and unsure of ourselves and our abilities, we do not perform very well. "Those with little conviction that they have the capacity to master their fate characteristically lack the motivation to even try," is the way James MacGregor Burns puts it. What we of course want for our leaders is that they will want to try, believing they can do yet better and wishing to overcome whatever barriers may stand in the way of the mission to which they and the organization are committed. That is the tone you want in your executive evaluation experience—one that produces energy and good forward action rather than draining, wearying and weakening enervation. Most all of us know and feel the difference and have in fact experienced it in our own lives. Your challenge is to recreate this energy in the experience of executive evaluation.

Getting to a better tone and starting place is neither mysterious nor complicated. It involves such things as simple trust and positive regard for your executive. You must believe that this person is in this job not because of the money, but because they care deeply about the mission; that they want to do well and are committed to the organization; and that they are interested in learning and, in fact, will do better at it with your encouragement.

We do, of course, understand that this is not true for some very small portion of the not-for-profit executive pool. But to approach the sensitive and important task of evaluation with only that small minority in mind, rather than the large majority of executives who are thoroughly committed, would be a serious mistake.

Perhaps then the ultimate test of the success of your executive evaluation is whether or not your executive comes away feeling clearer and more confident about your expectations; stronger and better able to face the unavoidable challenges in the life of your organization; more inspired to learn and grow professionally; and, more appreciative and trusting in the relationship among all those responsible for the leadership of your organization.

Having a Conversation

A very good place to begin considering executive evaluation is with a thoughtful conversation between the executive and the board or board committee. Two subjects that might form the basis for this conversation are: What will we call this thing? and What are our mutual expectations?

On Naming

We have struggles with words, and you should too. What is clear is that whatever you choose to call this experience with your executive will not mean at all the same thing to everyone. Is it evaluation, assessment, performance appraisal, performance review, some kind of rating or ranking, or something related to measuring or estimating, or even judging or grading? Reading back over the choices, it is not hard to imagine that someone will have an objection, even a strong negative reaction, to just about anything you choose.

We tend to prefer "review" disconnected from "performance." It has a neutral feel and when disassociated from performance loses the implication that performing is all (thought and integrity are less often captured in a performance-based approach.) We also favor "evaluation," partly because of its commonality, but mostly because buried in it are the words "value" and "valuing." That fits well with our notion of setting a good tone.

Most important is that you and your executive converse together to make a mutual decision about what you will call this thing that you will do together. It will be the first demonstration of your intent to bring clarity and respect to all involved in the process.

On Expectations

You will probably wish to reach a common understanding on a number of other expectations as well. In Chapter 5 (beginning on p. 22), we list what might be called the "organizationally based" issues of who should be involved, when it should happen, how often it should take place, what you will do with the results and what success will look like. But here we note for you some personal and process-related issues that might well be agreed upon before launching the evaluation. Again, the very act of having a preview evaluation conversation to discuss what both parties would like out of the experience reinforces a tone of mutual respect and greatly lessens the "powerful over the powerless," "this is the way it is going to go" attitude that would likely lead to a de-motivating evaluation.

You and your executive may wish to choose agenda items for your pre-evaluation conversation from the following:

1. What purposes do the committee and the executive believe the evaluation should serve? (See Chapter 4 for some ideas.)

2. What roles will the executive and the board president play in selecting the core evaluation committee?

3. What we will call this process? (See "On Naming," above)

4. How will we decide which inventory/process to utilize?

5. What is the right balance between executive self-evaluation and committee evaluation of the executive?

6. To what extent will this be a conversation-based review?

7. To what extent will some form of rating be made on each item prior to a conversation?

8. Should other board members be involved in some kind of rating without conversation?

9. What experiences about evaluation does each of us bring to this evaluation experience?

10. What are some of the things we would wish to avoid?

What this list suggests to us, and we hope to you as well, is that the pre-evaluation conversation is crucial, will take time and thought and, if done right, will go a long way toward ensuring a satisfactory executive evaluation experience.

Chapter 3
Crucial Considerations

Three more brief but important matters to think about before you begin designing your executive evaluation: the context for your evaluation (you are not doing this in a vacuum unrelated to the life of your organization); the not-for-profit culture (not nearly as much like the for-profit culture as you might think); and the message of your evaluation (you will be sending a message to your executive about such not-so-small matters as trust, power and belief).

The Context of Your Evaluation

While it may seem obvious, remember that whatever you do as a board needs to fit nicely under the protective umbrella of your mission statement—and this will be particularly true of executive evaluation. Can you recite your mission? Can you find where it is written down? Has your board looked at it critically in the past year? Does the language need freshening up or the focus sharpened? However you answer these questions, it would be a good thing to use the mission as the major touchstone from which you assemble the process of your executive evaluation. It could be that there are aspects of that mission that have faded or been bent by practices that would benefit from being part of the evaluation conversation.

Then, what about your strategic plan? Are you in the first year of a three-year plan or the final year of a two-year plan? Let's guess with all the talk about plans and accountability that you do have one. Let's also guess that it isn't exactly front and center at your board meetings (not unusual, you'll be happy to know). But let's hope that after a demanding board retreat and the difficulty of getting it down on paper that at least now you will drag it out and see what, if anything, it might suggest about the direction and context of the executive evaluation you are about to design. Once your evaluation experience has been considered in relation to both your mission and your strategic plan, it will feel much more grounded in the center of your organizational life—a very good place to be.

There are a number of other contextual matters that you may wish to ponder before proceeding:

- What is the general climate in your community about not-for-profit organizations? Is there pressure for greater accountability or transparency, additional social-entrepreneurial ventures, more exacting organizational ethics or yet something else?

- What about those who are your clients or audience? What are their concerns? What are they asking for, or perhaps demanding?

- What about those important constituents who provide you with funds: foundations, government agencies, corporations and individuals? What are they saying to you with their generosity (or lack thereof), or their written or off-the-record comments?

- What would you say are the three (not twelve, please) most pressing current issues or challenges for your organization?

- What would you say is the mood of your board? Are they engaged, generally involved and respectful of your executive? Do they show up, follow through and speak well of your organization in the community?

- What would you say is the mood of your executive? Does she or he seem to have energy and optimism about her or his work? Does she or he have good relationships with members of the staff and board? Does she or he take vacations, observe holidays, go home before dark?

There may well be other matters that come together to form the context within which you will carry out your executive evaluation. If you think a moment or two about them, they will inform what you decide to do with your executive evaluation, likely making it a more productive and satisfying experience for all.

The Not-for-profit Culture

Having people from the business sector on boards is a good thing. It is yet a better thing if they understand that the sector in which they work has a culture that is different from the not-for-profit sector in which they volunteer—not better or worse, just different. It would be a mistake to assume that because the for-profit sector has more money and, therefore, more power that it is intrinsically more valuable. Understanding and respecting the differences between for-profit and not-for-profit organizations is an important matter for those who sit on boards. When it comes to our subject of executive evaluation it is particularly important.

We see three key cultural differences with implications for the task of evaluation. They include differences in the approach to the bottom line; the importance of personal motivation; and the role of constituents in the decision-making process.

The Bottom Line Difference

While many of late have written about this difference, no one has done so with more clarity than Jim Collins. The *Good to Great* author has now written a book on how that concept applies to the social sector (see "Additional Reading," p. 49). He writes, "One of the primary differences between business and the social sectors [his phrase for not-for-profits] is that in business, money is both an input (a resource for achieving greatness) and an output (a measure of greatness). In the social sectors, money is only an input and not a measure of greatness."

This, of course, does not mean that in our not-for-profits money should not be carefully managed or utilized only for the mission, or that budgets should not be balanced. It does suggest that when we go about the task of evaluation we talk about money primarily in the context of resource generation. And that when we talk about success and outcomes we talk mostly of mission and programs.

Going back to Collins—when he differentiates between the business and social sectors on the issue of defining and measuring "great," he expands upon the above quote in this way: "In the business sector there is a widely agreed upon financial metric of performance. Money is both an input (a means to success) and an output (a measure of success). In the social sectors there are fewer widely agreed-upon metrics of performance. Money is only an input, not an output. Performance relative to mission, not financial returns, is the primary definition of success."

This fairly major difference needs to be taken into consideration as you think about what you will focus on, value and attempt to measure in your not-for-profit executive evaluation.

The Personal Motivation Difference

Perhaps the best and clearest statement on the for-profit/not-for-profit difference regarding personal motivation is by Peter Block (see "Additional Reading," p. 49). Reporting on a study done on workforce satisfaction, he writes in the *Nonprofit Quarterly*,

> "People in the nonprofit sector are pursuing work that has a compelling purpose, high social value and offers strong personal meaning...[This] leads to the second obvious truth about nonprofit work: there is not much money in it...For a nonprofit manager this combination of meaningful work and meager resources is a good thing. You have highly motivated people, who by and large respect their own work, their own organization and the people around them. And, you get all this for a bargain. Best of all you have people who make a decent living, but know they are not going to get rich."

This analysis points to yet another important aspect of not-for-profit culture vital to doing effective executive evaluation.

Few of us need an author to tell us that the decision-making process in for-profits is largely different from that in not-for-profits. We have all experienced the slowness of not-for-profit decision making, even been frustrated by it. But we are not, surprisingly, inclined to think of it as cumbersome and ineffective. Staff, board, committees and sometimes external agents all need to be included in the process. The danger and downside lie in the length of time it takes and the painful negotiation of consensus out of difference. The advantages are in the inclusiveness and ownership it creates, and how many times a more complete solution is found after having integrated the insights of so many.

The for-profit CEO, in contrast, has authority in most situations to make the decision and get on with it. The advantage of decisiveness and speed is obvious. Less obvious is the still-attendant need to then "sell" the decision and its results to others. Less obvious as well is that in the subsequent selling and explaining, information often emerges that requires the decision to be amended. Worse, vital information from the broader group is too often disregarded in the drive for efficiency, control or both.

In short, the cultures are different around the executive's role in decision making, and there are advantages and disadvantages to the process in each of the cultures. For your purposes, those differences and those advantages and disadvantages need to be well in your mind as you go about the task of executive evaluation in the not-for-profit sector. What your executive is able to do, given multiple constituent considerations, is different. What your executive must be skilled at doing given those considerations is vital.

The Message of Your Evaluation

Our flyers send messages, our web sites send messages and so do our press releases, advertisements, logo and graphics. Most of us know and understand that about our organizations in this age of branding. Less obvious but no less powerful are the messages we send by such common things as the way we go about recruiting and selecting board members, recruiting and hiring staff and, our subject here, the way we choose to do executive evaluation. And while those messages do not go out to a broad community audience, they are heard clearly by the ones with whom we have entrusted the leadership of our organization and who, however discreetly, do talk with other colleagues, consultants, family and friends.

So what are we saying with the way we do executive evaluation? It's worth thinking about. Here are the actions and implied messages we most often hear about from the executives we know:

Action I: No board member was designated to take the lead in executive evaluation, no time was set or allowed, and no idea was presented about how to proceed.

Executive Hears: This must not be that important to them.

Action II: Board president called and made an appointment to talk over what the executive would hope for in an evaluation experience.

Executive Hears: These people care about and support me.

Action III: A board member brought in an assessment form from his office and had the personnel committee fill it out on the executive, then called the executive in and announced the results.

Executive Hears: These people like to be the boss rather than colleagues, or at least are comfortable only when they are in control.

Action IV: The board and the executive agreed on a form to use, with one-to-five rankings on each of twenty-two executive functions and skills. The board committee and executive all filled one out and then shared the scores in the context of a conversation about what the numbers meant and where they were different and similar.

Executive Hears: These people understand that a big part of this is strengthening our mutual understanding, even our relationship, and not just giving some abstract grade.

Action V: The evaluation was called an annual review, but the only thing reviewed was salary, cost of living and what other people made in similar jobs.

Executive Hears: They don't understand me. They think money is the only thing here. They don't get it that I really want to know how I'm doing, how I can be better and what more I should be learning about.

You may or may not be sending any of the above messages. But you are sending *some* kind of message, like it or not. The question is, is that the message you wish to send—is that what you want to communicate to your executive? If it is, good for you. If it is not, well, better think about it all some more.

Section Two

Now Comes Design

Chapter 4

Evaluation Purposes:
Clarity, Breadth and Depth

Another cartoon. Another large boss (is it true that they all are or do they just seem that way?) stares across the desk at a small, hapless man. "Ok, Smithers, we've got twelve minutes to agree on what was your fault last year." This starts the chapter on "Performance without Appraisal" in Peter Scholtes' splendid *The Leader's Handbook: Making Things Happen, Getting Things Done*. Executive evaluation fault-finding would be at the low-to-primitive end of Scholtes' scale. And the hurried-up feel of twelve minutes would certainly result in little of value, whatever the stated purpose.

Arriving at a stated purpose, actually *clarified* and *broadened* purposes, is what this section is all about. Three things at the outset: there are many purposes for executive evaluation; they are not mutually exclusive; and you and your executive should decide together which ones to pursue in your design of an evaluation experience.

We have chosen to highlight five potential purposes. Our hope is that some of them will expand your view of what can be accomplished in an executive evaluation. Our suggestion is that you review these five, have a conversation about them with your board and executive to reach an initial agreement about where you would like to begin, and then try to organize your own evaluation experience around that. (Some tips for how to do that organizing are presented in the next chapter, "Evaluation Details.") We end this chapter with the matter of salary review—which we believe is necessary, although a different and separate matter from evaluation.

So here are five purposes that your executive evaluation could encompass: executive oversight, professional development, looking forward, advancing a culture of reflection and strengthening collegiality.

Executive Oversight

This is a purpose perhaps more often associated with for-profit than not-for-profit organizations. While nonprofit boards may not wish to use phrases like "monitor the work of" or "manage the work of," it is true that insofar as an executive has a "boss" or someone to whom to report, it is the board.

The trick is to carry out this oversight role in a knowledgeable, thoughtful way that minimizes intrusiveness and authoritarian attitudes. Over fifty years ago Douglas MacGregor wrote in his landmark book *The Human Side of Enterprise*, "When performance appraisal is perceived as a technique of personnel administration…it becomes a part of a managerial strategy, the implicit logic of which is to get people to direct their efforts toward organizational objectives…[meaning that] management must tell them what to do, judge how well they have done and reward or punish them accordingly."

In our view this would not be a healthy or productive system to instill and perpetuate. While the board does have the responsibility to review the work of the executive, to do so in a 1950s industrial model would be less than desirable. Such a system reinforces hierarchy, diminishes the executive and suggests that the relationship between board and executive is one based primarily on power and mistrust. If the relationship has actually deteriorated to that point, it is likely to be time to remove some of the actors—and that would include not only the executive but some of those on the board side as well.

We believe that the board's oversight function can and should lead it to enter into regular conversations about roles (board and executive) and focus (what are the priorities) without lapsing into a mode of paternalistic management. In fact there are tools (which we suggest beginning on p. 29), that can assist with the "role and focus" conversation and do so in a way that engenders trust and respect among those entrusted with the leadership of the organization. Particularly, you may wish to look at:

#1   **Leadership Roles and Competencies**

#4   **Inventory of Leadership Attributes and Abilities**

#5   **Leading and Managing: Conversations on the Difference**

#9   **An Annual Assessment Instrument**

#10   **Core Components for Success**

#12   **Contracting for Effectiveness**

#14   **Analysis of Pressing Issues**

Professional Development

Here's one that is hard to be against and if done right has nothing but positive in it for everyone. What executive would not want their board to encourage and support their professional development and what board would not want an executive who was on the lookout for learning? Our experience is that this works best when the board is more in a "how can we assist" mode than a "here's what you need to learn and how you ought to do it" mode. In our view the movement should always be in the direction of self-directed, not other-directed, learning. Executives need to be encouraged to fully graduate from the "teacher knows best" style. As adult learners, executives need to be pointed toward, and encouraged in, a self-reflective process of asking, "What do I need to know and be able to do and how am I going to learn it?"

Boards can and should participate with the executive in identifying an agenda for professional development. They can even assist in structuring it and identifying sources for it. What they probably should not do is take away the executive's initiative and begin to be in charge of the learning of another adult. In addition, while much professional development can result from reading and informal peer discussion, boards can also see that some funds are made available for professional seminars and conferences.

The professional development purpose for the evaluation experience can particularly be served by utilizing the following tools (see p. 29):

#1   **Leadership Roles and Competencies**

#3   **Exemplary Leadership Practices**

#4   **Inventory of Leadership Attributes and Abilities**

#5   **Leading and Managing: Conversations on the Difference**

#8   **"The Trouble with Leaders" Inventory**

Looking Forward in the Short Term

Traditionally, executive evaluation has meant looking at the past and assessing what kinds of learning can benefit the future. A majority of the processes and tools we suggest do just that. Sometimes, however, getting a handle on the immediate future can be a strong approach for executive development. You may decide that this is merely short-term planning. Whatever it is or whatever it is called, insofar as executive evaluation is about assisting leaders to do better and to be more effective and productive, this can help.

Again, our experience is that when the board and executive define a short-term focus *together*, it works better. Assignments that come from the board to the executive, while not always to be avoided, in this case tend to work less well. If this is one of your purposes you may wish to utilize the following tools (see p. 29):

#4   **Inventory of Leadership Attributes and Abilities**

#11   **Key Relationships: For Review and Development**

#12   **Contracting for Effectiveness**

#14   **Analysis of Pressing Issues**

Advancing a Culture of Reflection

Most organizations are too much of the time in a "decide quickly and act now" mode. While there are certainly more than a few circumstances that warrant that approach, it can easily become a habitual way of working to the long term detriment of the organization. Thinking time…reflecting time…is hard to come by. Board meetings tend to be filled with reports to be heard and business to be done. Staff meetings are largely filled with updates to be shared and problems to be solved. Of course one must attend to reports, updates and problems. We would like to argue strongly, however, for reflection, for closing the door, for feet up on the desk. We advocate as well for asking significant questions at board meetings—big enough and deep enough questions to warrant thirty minutes' worth of thoughtful conversation.

Sometimes the executive evaluation can be a way into that reflective mode. Rather than one more hurried task to do, it can be time set aside to ponder. Rather than one item on a long list to check off, it can be a time to think about the list itself and what is worthy of being there. In short, if you wish to have an organizational culture with built-in reflection and quiet conversation time, consider how to make time for reflection part of your executive evaluation. If you do, our guess is that it will become contagious. Try it particularly with the following tools (see p. 29):

#5   **Leading and Managing: Conversations on the Difference**

#6   **Conversations About Leadership: Inspired by Literature**

#7   **Conversations About Leadership: Inspired by Gurus**

#8   **"The Trouble with Leaders" Inventory**

#13   **Assessing Personal Satisfaction**

#15   **Conversations About Leadership: Inspired by Philosophy and Social Science**

Strengthening Collegiality

An unfortunate and far too common phenomenon in not-for-profit organizations is that the board and executive fall out of open, trusting communication and into mistrust bordering on an adversarial state. Of course, when this is going on at the core of the organization among top leadership positions, it has no small effect on everyone and everything else. It is, therefore, particularly important that the executive and board leadership exemplify a way of being together that they hope will characterize the committee, staff and volunteer relationships throughout the organization.

As all of us have experienced personally and professionally, such exemplary relationships do not just magically come about. They take work and they take periods of time when that work can get done. One of our executive colleagues says that a part of her job is to see that the board members have a satisfying experience engaged in something of significance to the mission they signed up to hold in trust. We would add that it is also part of the job of the board to see that the executive has a satisfying experience, significantly engaged in the organizational mission he signed up to give his work-life to. It is that level of attention to the other in this leadership partnership that sets the stage for things to go well. If part (or even most) of leading is about serving, a board and executive who can get in that serving mode toward one another are going to create the kind of organization where you want to be.

One way to get to that good place is to use an executive evaluation whose purposes include strengthening the partnership among those who lead. Among the fifteen evaluation tools contained in Chapter 7 (beginning on p. 29) are a few evaluation processes that will move you toward that goal. We would particularly call your attention to:

#3   **Exemplary Leadership Practices**

#5   **Leading and Managing: Conversations on the Difference**

#7   **Conversations About Leadership: Inspired by Gurus**

#8   **"The Trouble with Leaders" Inventory**

#11   **Key Relationships for Review and Development**

#13   **Assessing Personal Satisfaction**

Salary Review Approaches and Resources

In many organizations this seems to be the primary reason there is a once-a-year conversation at all, sometimes called something like performance review or executive evaluation. It is a good and fair thing for the board to review the compensation of the executive annually. We believe, however, that that fairly straightforward, matter-of-fact conversation is better done in isolation from the broader purposes of professional evaluation. Since it is generally not easy to have a conversation about money, our belief is that if it is also connected to a conversation about learning and professional development, the whole will surely not go well. That is to say the executive will not walk away feeling empowered, motivated and inspired to do the leadership job with more wisdom and skill.

Try this. Connect the annual salary review to the budgeting process, not the evaluation or appraisal process. That means if the budget is due at the December board meeting, the salary review should happen in October. Second, untangle that conversation about compensation from the evaluation conversation about professional development role and organizational focus. Having the power of money on the table usually produces defensiveness and even contentiousness—not a good atmosphere for hearing important messages and making needed changes.

What if, instead, the salary review decisions were made primarily in reference to a few basic pieces of financial information? Take a look at the consumer price index. How has it changed over the past year, and wouldn't you at least want your executive's salary to keep pace with that indicator?

Next, what are the salary norms in your marketplace? Specifically, what do not-for-profits of your size, in your region, in your sector pay their executives? Be careful: Omaha is different than Boston; a three million dollar budget is something different from a three hundred thousand dollar one; and health care pays differently than youth-serving agencies.

To avail yourself of the consumer price index and the norms of the marketplace, we suggest the following resources:

One excellent resource for not-for-profit organizations is GuideStar, at http://www.guidestar.org. GuideStar's mission is to "revolutionize philanthropy and nonprofit practice with information." This mission is accomplished by providing searchable data on more than one-and-a-half million not-for-profit organizations, collected from their Form 990s and supplementary information. With a free membership, you can access the 990 of any not-for-profit included on GuideStar's site. So if you want to compare your executive's salary with organizations you deem similar, you could find those figures easily. GuideStar also offers national, regional and state compensation reports for a fee.

Another on-line resource you might find useful is made available by Abbott, Langer & Associates (http://www.abbott-langer.com). Located in Chicago, Abbott Langer offers comprehensive reports organized by sector and/or profession that are derived from salary and benefits surveys, including the report *Compensation in Nonprofit Organizations*. While a fee is required to access the full report, some information is available for free in the summary data.

Other great sources for normative data are available only in hardcopy or with subscriptions. A reference publication that is extremely useful is the ACCRA Cost of Living Index, which breaks down the cost of living in the United States by metropolitan area; it is published by the American Chamber of Commerce Researchers Association on a quarterly basis. Also available is the American Salaries and Wages Survey. This survey gives more than 40,000 salary statistics for various occupations and includes information on the type of work; industry; location; low, mid and high figures; and the dates and sources of the information. Another excellent resource is the Economic Research Institute, which maintains a competitive salary survey that includes cost-of-living information. ERI offers several types of databases and even one specifically about nonprofit executive compensation.

The Bureau of Labor and Statistics' web site (http://www.bls.gov) has extensive information on everything from the official U.S. Consumer Price Index (http://www.bls.gov/cpi/home.htm) to the National Compensation Survey. The National Compensation Survey includes an area called "Regional Resources" that allows you to select your state (and some large metro areas), so that you can compare your executive's salary with the norm for similar professions in your area (http://www.bls.gov/ncs/ocs/compub.htm). The BLS site even includes a step-by-step process for appraising pay called "The Guide for Evaluating Your Firm's Jobs and Pay" (http://www.bls.gov/ncs/ocs/sp/ncbr0004.pdf).

You may be able to access these fee-based resources for free through your public library. Depending on the library system, card holders may even have access to subscription databases. Check with your local library's reference desk for details.

Finally (almost), take a look at the recent history of your salary and benefits package. If it has not changed or changed only a little, it may be time to do something. We understand that "do something" could either mean adjust upward or move to terminate. The latter is certainly more honestly and humanely done through direct conversation than through the backhanded message of a long-stagnant salary. Organizations, even boards, do get reputations and that is one you don't want to get in your community.

Finally (really), there are intangible though powerful judgments like, Is your board just crazy about the executive and her work? Does your board want to make a strong statement that this is an executive you do not want to lose? If the answers are yes or even mostly yes, that would of course argue for a positive change in compensation beyond the consumer price index and beyond what is average for your size, sector and location.

Chapter 5

Evaluation Details:
The Who, When and What of It

They say (well, someone says), "It's all in the details." And, in fact, there are a few particular details that may not individually make your evaluation experience but could certainly break it if you and your executive do not reach an agreement on them in advance. We would now like to call them to your attention and say a brief word about each. In order, they are: Who should be involved? When and how often should evaluation happen? What will you do with the results? What are the most common errors? And what will success look like?

Who Should Be Involved?

The answer to who should be involved depends on what involvement means. Our own preference is that the executive, plus a few designated board members and, later, the whole board, should always be fully engaged. Sometimes, with some evaluation processes, you may wish to add staff and other insiders (e.g., past board presidents), but this involvement would be selective and partial. Finally, once in a while you may find it important to gather information from important outsiders (major funders, constituents and community leaders). Again, their involvement would be limited and carefully orchestrated.

Back to the board and executive. There is no one best way for them to work together, but let us describe one format that we have seen work well. The board president and executive meet and agree on three board members who know the organization well, are good at open, thoughtful and straightforward communication and are somewhat representative of the membership of the whole board. This evaluation committee, which may or may not include the board president, meets with the executive to have those important pre-evaluation conversations, clarifying the purposes they all wish to address, going over the details described in this section and reviewing and selecting the tool or process most likely to serve their agreed-upon purposes. If the tool lends itself to full board participation up front, then the entire board is included at that stage. If not, the committee and executive proceed through the process, reach whatever preliminary conclusions seem agreeable and then engage the full board in a discussion of these preliminary opinions. The board is free to add or to amend before a final, written statement is made.

This model, while mostly manageable, requires a fairly major commitment of time and energy. That is why we suggest that you only add others (staff or outsiders) with great care and for some particularly compelling reason. Once added at the front end, they will naturally want to hear results and even wish to be involved in shaping them. This can quickly become unwieldy.

When and How Often Should Evaluation Happen?

Let's do the second half of this question first. If you break out salary review, as we suggest, and link it to the budgeting process instead, then we would say once or twice a year. Some of the tools and processes you may choose will lend themselves to six month intervals; others work fine on an annual basis. So sometimes the tool will determine the frequency, while, at other times, the general pace of the organization or whether or not this executive has ever *had* an evaluation will suggest an answer of either once or twice a year.

The "when" needs to fit in with your budgeting and programming season. What times in your typical year imply new beginnings (September? January?), or what times are less hurried and lend themselves to reflection, perhaps early summer or spring? The most important thing is to get it on the calendar and be able to count on it year in and year out.

What Will You Do with the Results?

The simple answer is to record them, keep them safely for reference, and share them only with those whom the executive and board can agree upon. In general, the evaluation experience is for insiders. Whether it be used primarily as a guide for professional development, focusing future leadership activity or strengthening the partnership between board and executive, it is intended for that core group of people who comprise the leadership team in your organization. The most crucial thing is that that group should engage deeply and fully understand the results. They may or may not find some strategic or public relations reason to communicate more broadly with other constituents.

What are the Most Common Errors?

For what it is worth, here are the top ten mistakes we encounter that can easily undermine all the good intentions and hard work of evaluations:

1. The board communicates that evaluation is not important by failing to initiate the process or take it seriously.

2. The expectations are not clear and/or agreed upon.

3. Too little time is allocated to do the process thoughtfully.

4. The wrong people get involved. Wrong would be those who have an axe to grind or are not representative of the majority point of view of the board.

5. The evaluation committee plays boss and reinforces a power-focused, hierarchical way of thinking.

6. Contextual issues are not taken into consideration (e.g., the life stage of the organization or significant forces in the environment).

7. The ratio between talking and listening is skewed greatly toward talking.

8. The ratio between asking good questions and making opinion-heavy statements is skewed greatly toward the latter.

9. There is a lack of discipline about sticking to the agreed-upon evaluation process.

10. The follow-up discussion and tracking are weak or nonexistent.

What Will Success Look Like: Evaluating the Evaluation

Success will be the board coming away from the experience feeling that they better understand the executive, that their attention and encouragement will result in her growth and development and that their partnership with the executive has been strengthened for the betterment of the organization.

Success will be the executive coming away from the experience feeling better known and understood, supported and encouraged in his own professional development, more confident that the partnership with the board is healthy and productive, and reassured that all parties are well able to exercise their own leadership in the organization.

You may wish to come up with your own list of indicators of success. Perhaps you will want to include measures that are more quantifiable, but those measurements and criteria will need to be agreed upon in advance. It is our belief, however, that regardless of what other measures you choose to utilize, if the conditions described above for the board and executive are not achieved, few other measures are worth the discussion.

Section Three

Then Comes Action

Chapter 6

Shaping the Process, Selecting an Inventory

We are about to deluge you with lots of choices. How will you decide? First of all, there are probably at least three processes that would work just fine for you, so don't spend too much time looking for the single perfect one. Second, think back over some of the conclusions you were beginning to reach as you read Section One ("First Comes Thought") and Section Two ("Now Comes Design"). You might wish to focus particularly on three matters to help narrow your choices. The starting place of shared expectations and understandings with your executive is a good place to begin. You may also have the strong contextual frame of a recent strategic plan or newly created position description to point you toward one tool or another. Finally, it's a smart thing to clarify once more the purpose(s) that you wish the evaluation to serve. Several are mentioned in Chapter 4 and you may have thought of others.

Next is the issue of exactly who will make your decision. Probably the executive, board president and head of the personnel committee ought to be in on it—and maybe others. The others would include anyone else who has been selected to be part of the core evaluation team of two to four. You may wish to have them each review the list of approaches, choose their two to three favorites and then compare those choices. The final decision may emerge simply and quickly. If not, remember you'll be doing this again in three to six months, so rather than struggle over a consensus, pick one for now and another for later. You will have to decide the extent to which you need to have the whole board involved at this point. Since, presumably, they have selected you to make the choice of a tool, let them know in advance of the evaluation what choice has been made and why.

If you want to get really creative, you may wish to combine parts of one tool with parts of another. For example, some might like very clear lists of specific skill items combined with a few more general, open-ended, reflective questions. In any case, it is yours to decide, yours to try out, yours to amend and yours to try another next time. Whatever you do, make sure everyone involved benefits from it with new learnings, stronger relationships and a better sense of direction for the board and executive leadership of the organization.

In whatever you choose, the key is providing time for thoughtful conversation. This is particularly true if you decide to use numeric rankings. A 3.5 without conversation about what that means is less than useful. Equally important is an emphasis upon the executive's increased capacity to have self-awareness about the item being evaluated. Most agree that our own self-assessment about any attribute or ability is the best motivator for learning and betterment.

Previewing Some Evaluation Options

Option 1 – Leadership Roles and Competencies

Based on the work of Robert Quinn, this approach utilizes characteristics of eight roles executives will likely have to assume in their leadership. These form the basis for a conversation between the board and the executive about which roles come naturally and which require conscious attention.

Option 2 – The Making of an Effective Executive

Peter Drucker claims that all effective executives follow eight leadership practices that include planning, actions and attitudes. This approach lists these eight practices for boards and executives to explore together.

Option 3 – Exemplary Leadership Practices

James Kouzes and Barry Posner studied exemplary leaders and identified five practices that were constant among them. Considering these practices may assist in assessing the primary leadership efforts of the executive. Each of the practices is further differentiated by two commitments.

Option 4 – Inventory of Leadership Attributes and Abilities

This inventory includes twenty-two attributes and abilities identified by agency executives and board presidents as crucial for effective leadership. They range from self awareness to bringing out the best in others, with a dual focus on action and process.

Option 5 – Leading and Managing: Conversations on the Difference

This approach visually contrasts the roles and actions of a manager versus a leader, assisting the board and executive to consciously determine which mode is most preferred in the present organizational situation.

Option 6 – Conversations About Leadership: Inspired by Literature

Often boards and executives learn the most from and about each other by talking indirectly about their partnership in less formal conversations. This approach uses literary quotations related to leadership as an indirect way to talk about matters of import to the leaders of the organization.

Option 7 – Conversations About Leadership: Inspired by Gurus

Like "Conversations About Leadership: Inspired by Literature," this approach uses quotations to start conversations. Here the sources of inspiration are the premier thinkers on leadership studies. Use our quotes or add your own favorites in order to have significant conversations about organizational leadership.

Option 8 – "The Trouble with Leaders" Inventory

Developed out of a conversation among four leadership gurus, this inventory highlights eight problems with American leadership. Each statement begins with, "The trouble with American leaders..." The statements help boards and executives focus on the state of community leadership, with strong implications for organizational leadership.

Option 9 – An Annual Assessment Instrument

This fully comprehensive, more traditional approach provides a form for evaluators to rank the executive's performance. The six different categories include programming, human resources, community relations, finances, fundraising and board of directors. Developed collaboratively by BoardSource and CompassPoint.

Option 10 – Core Components for Success

This approach is appealing for its simplicity, which encourages high participation in the evaluation process. It is visually straightforward. The one-page form asks respondents to rate and comment on nine essential abilities for leadership. The responses are then summarized to form the basis for a conversation.

Option 11 – Key Relationships for Review and Development

Some would say that leadership is mostly about relationships. This approach focuses on the primary relationships the executive maintains inside and outside the organization. Space is provided not only to indicate the status of the relationship but also to list ideas for improvement and factors that strengthen or subvert.

Option 12 – Contracting for Effectiveness

Contracting for Effectiveness utilizes substantial board and executive involvement to set short-term leadership goals in each of five categories. While it requires a considerable commitment of energy and time, it offers the possibility to establish clearly focused, highly desirable and achievable goals.

Option 13 – Assessing Personal Satisfaction

If the goal of your organization is to improve the quality of life for your community, then shouldn't this be the case for those most closely associated with the organization as well? This approach looks at the satisfaction of both board and executive to foster a healthy organizational culture, which in turn is more likely to perform in ways that provide the highest benefits for your target audience.

Option 14 – Analysis of Pressing Issues

This approach provides assistance with short- and long-term priorities for the organization and the executive. There are always plenty of issues and more than enough good things to do—this is one way to assist the board and staff leadership in focusing on the most important and putting off or even refusing to pursue the less important.

Option 15 – Conversations About Leadership: Inspired by Philosophy and Social Science

Springboards for significant conversations can come from anywhere, including philosophers and social scientists. From Aristotle to Martin Luther King, Jr., these quotes are sure to lead to an interesting conversation between the board and executive about core leadership issues.

Chapter 7

Fifteen Options
to Consider

Option 1 – Leadership Roles and Competencies

This process grows out of the work of Robert Quinn, a professor in the University of Michigan Graduate School of Business with extensive firsthand experience in not-for-profit organizations. (Two of his fine books are listed in the "Additional Reading" section that starts on p. 49.)

Quinn describes eight distinct managerial leadership roles that pretty much all executives need to perform at a fairly advanced level. The most general way to use this approach is to have the executive and the evaluation committee identify the roles in which each feels the executive is strongest and those which need to be brought more into the center of the executive's work life.

In more detail, you could have a good conversation about each role and its attending competencies, with or without prior rating on a five-point scale for effectiveness.

Mentor Role	1. Understanding self and others 2. Communicating effectively 3. Developing subordinates
Facilitator Role	1. Building teams 2. Using participative decision-making 3. Managing conflict
Monitor Role	1. Monitoring individual performance 2. Managing collective performance 3. Managing organizational performance
Coordinator Role	1. Managing projects 2. Designing work 3. Managing across functions
Director Role	1. Visioning, planning and goal setting 2. Designing and organizing 3. Delegating effectively
Producer Role	1. Working productively 2. Fostering a productive work environment 3. Managing time and stress
Broker Role	1. Building and maintaining a power base 2. Negotiating agreement and commitment 3. Presenting ideas
Innovator Role	1. Living with change 2. Thinking creatively 3. Creating change

Option 2 – The Making of an Effective Executive

While this particular list first appeared in the *Harvard Business Review*, Peter Drucker has written often and wisely about not-for-profit leadership. As one of the fathers of American management science, he has studied the personalities, attitudes, values, strengths and weaknesses of leaders in all sectors.

He believes that leaders who are truly effective follow the following eight practices. The first two practices give them the knowledge they need; the next four help them convert this knowledge into effective action; and the last two ensure that the whole organization feels responsible and accountable.

Use all eight as points to begin a conversation. Ask which ones are practiced well or less well. Or make up a rating chart for each—you decide.

1. Effective leaders: Ask, "What needs to be done?"

2. Ask, "What is right for the enterprise?"

3. Develop action plans.

4. Take responsibility for decisions.

5.` Take responsibility for communicating.

6. Focus on opportunities rather than problems.

7. Run productive meetings.

8. Think and say "we" rather than "I."

Chapter 7: Fifteen Options to Consider

Option 3 – Exemplary Leadership Practices

The fine researchers and writers James Kouzes and Barry Posner identified and studied leaders who were exemplary. They concluded that all had five distinct practices that were central to their way of leading, each accompanied by two strong and constant commitments.

These thought-provoking identifiers provide an opportunity for significant discussion with your executive. As with other evaluation approaches, each identifier may also be assessed as a strength or a challenge, with or without a rating scale.

Model the Way

1. Find your voice by clarifying your personal values.

2. Set the example by aligning actions with shared values.

Inspire a Shared Vision

3. Envision the future by imagining exciting and ennobling possibilities.

4. Enlist others in a common vision by appealing to shared aspirations.

Challenge the Process

5. Search for opportunities by seeking innovative ways to change, grow and improve.

6. Experiment and take risks by constantly generating small wins and learning from mistakes.

Enable Others to Act

7. Foster collaboration by promoting cooperative goals and building trust.

8. Strengthen others by sharing power and discretion.

Encourage the Heart

9. Recognize contributions by showing appreciation for individual excellence.

10. Celebrate values and victories by creating a spirit of community.

Option 4 – Inventory of Leadership Attributes and Abilities

This listing of twenty-two attributes and abilities resulted from interviews with funding agency executives and board presidents. They were each asked to think of one or two of their most highly regarded executives and then describe what made them so effective.

This inventory is designed to be tailored to the needs of your organization. You first decide if an item is presently of importance to your organization. If it is not, then the performance of the executive in it need not be ranked. If it is very important, then you and the executive may check whether or not it needs to be strengthened. It is important here to have a conversation about the exact nature of what needs strengthening.

Attributes and Abilities	Very Important To My Organization	Of Little Importance	Performance Satisfactory	Performance Needs Strengthening
Understand the broader system in which organization must function				
Identify and respond appropriately to major constituents of organization				
Set the organizational agenda in the context of broader community issues and needs				
Identify and select competent staff & board members				
Assist staff & board in developing a common sense of mission				
Establish & maintain productive staff & board relations				
Utilize & develop talents of staff & board				
Assist staff & board in responding effectively to problems & opportunities				
Identify & clarify problems & opportunities for the organization				
Establish an organizational climate that minimizes the need for winners & losers				

Attributes and Abilities	Very Important To My Organization	Of Little Importance	Performance Satisfactory	Performance Needs Strengthening
Develop strategies that head off problems/crises before they occur				
Engage in consensus building & coalition forming				
Position, package & present organization well to community				
Design appropriate strategies for implementing organization's programs				
Conceptualize & articulate a vision & mission for organization				
Move consistently & effectively toward long-term goals				
Help organization evolve naturally with a minimum of false starts				
Sense when organization needs to move to a new phase or stage				
Uphold & maintain high performance standards for self & colleagues				
Indentify limits of own knowledge & skills & seek appropriate assistance				
Know when & where to take a stand				

Option 5 – Leading and Managing:
Conversations on the Difference

Most executives must involve themselves with practices related to management as well as those related to leadership. Some might say we need executives with greater leadership ability, while others would advocate for greater management ability. It is for you in your organization with your particular cast of staff and board characters to make that determination.

What follows is a list of ten items that contrast leadership behavior with management behavior. They might form the basis for determining how your executive tends to proceed, as well as what approaches are most needed given your present organizational situation. See *The Guru Guide* (listed in "Additional Reading" on p. 49) for more items.

Manager Approach	Leader Approach	What We Have	What We Need
Administer	Innovate		
Maintain	Develop		
Focus on systems	Focus on people		
Rely on control	Rely on trust		
Organize and staff	Align people with a direction		
Emphasize strategies, tactics and structure	Emphasize philosophy, values and goals		
Have a short-term focus	Have a long-term focus		
Ask how and when	Ask what and why		
Seek predictability and order	Seek change		
Require others to comply	Inspire others to follow		

Option 6 – Conversations About Leadership: Inspired by Literature

Depending upon your point of view, this approach will seem either wildly creative and insightful or at least a little unusual. You of course must be the judge. Our own experience is that oftentimes a literary quotation can lead to a richer, deeper and more multifaceted conversation about a leadership attribute than the mere listing of that attribute. For example, you might say, "Let's talk about the issue of verbal and written communication." Or you might read together the Mark Twain quote "The difference between the right word and the almost right word is the difference between lightning and the lightning bug." We believe that you and your executive need not be told that this quote has a lot to do with communication and is likely to lead to further useful conversation about that issue. We also would not presume to tell you that the Carlos Fuentes quote is related to comfort with diversity or that the Tom Robbins quote has something to do with courage and risk taking.

Here's the list. Start your conversation on any one of them. You may wish to direct the conversation toward reviewing and assessing the leadership quality suggested by the quote, or you may decide to just start the conversation prompted by the quote and see where it leads.

1. "...If anything I do in the way of writing novels isn't about the village or the community; then it is not about anything." —Toni Morrison

2. "The question of this decade is how do we deal with people who are not like us." —Carlos Fuentes

3. "...Heartfelt ineptitude has its appeal and so does heartless skill, but what you want is passionate virtuosity." —John Barth

4. "Imagination creates the situation and then the situation creates imagination." —James Baldwin

5. "Going to Walden is not so easy a thing as a green visit. It is the slow and difficult trick of living and finding it where you are." —Mary Oliver

6. "The difference between the right word and the almost right word is the difference between lightning and the lightning bug." —Mark Twain

7. "There is always an enormous temptation in all of life to diddle about making itsy bitsy friends and meals and journeys...We are making hay when we should be making whoopee; we are raising tomatoes when we should be raising Cain or Lazarus." —Annie Dillard

8. "...Real courage is risking something that might force you to rethink your thoughts and suffer change and stretch consciousness. Real courage is risking one's clichés." —Tom Robbins

9. "Beat your megaphones into ear trumpets." —William Stafford

10. "We do not deal much in facts when we are contemplating ourselves." —Mark Twain

Option 7 – Conversations About Leadership: Inspired by Gurus

In the world of leadership and management, as in most fields, there are gurus. These are the wise worthies who are usually beyond middle age and whose research, practice, writing or some combination of the three have made people pay attention. We have collected quotations on key leadership issues from a variety of these gurus. We present them as statements that are likely to provoke useful conversation between board members and executives. Again, we will not presume to tell you what key issues are embedded in the quotes. We leave that exploration, discovery and resulting significant conversation to you and your colleagues.

As with the leadership quotes, you may utilize each quote to assess the leadership quality suggested by it, or you may choose to have a more open-ended, exploratory conversation.

1. "The first and last task of leaders is to keep hope alive—despite the day's bitter discouragements, despite the perplexities of social action, despite our own shallowness or wavering resolve." —John W. Gardner

2. "So the point is not to become a leader, the point is to become yourself." —Warren Bennis

3. "The leader of the past was a person who knew how to tell. The leader of the future will be a person who knows how to ask." —Peter Drucker

4. "The goal is to balance a life that works with a life that counts...Just because something works, it doesn't mean that it matters." —Peter Block

5. "What we have before us is breathtaking opportunities disguised as insoluble problems." —John W. Gardner

6. "This then is the deeper territory of leadership—collectively listening to what is wanting to emerge in the world, and then having the courage to do what is required." —Joseph Jaworski

7. "We are not victims of society, we are its co-creators. The great insight of our spiritual traditions is that external reality does not impinge upon us as a prison or as an ultimate constraint. Instead, we co-create that reality." —Parker Palmer

8. "Perhaps the greatest challenge anyone in leadership faces is to bring one's public self as close as one can to the private self and vice versa. The aim is to cultivate a type of authenticity in one's behavior, an integration that offers resilience and strength to all one's efforts." —Carol Becker

9. "Beneath the surface of most constituencies are dormant volcanoes of emotion and motivation. The greatest leaders have always given expression to the unexpressed, have always had transactions with the hidden element in the souls of their audience." —John W. Gardner

10. "If a work is mine to do, it will make me glad over the long haul, despite the difficult days. Even the difficult days ultimately gladden me because they pose the kind of problems that help me grow in a work if it is truly mine." —Parker Palmer

Option 8 – "The Trouble with Leaders" Inventory

Joe Jaworski tells the story of trying to establish a curriculum that would develop leaders. As a first step, a group (Warren Bennis, Tom Cronin and Harlan Cleveland) sat down and tried to outline the problems that might be addressed in such a program. The answer took the form of eight propositions, each of which spelled out a problem with American leaders. We think it is good, largely accurate and very suggestive of important conversations that ought to be had today. It quite naturally suggests board-executive reflection on the eight principles of leadership, most of which are likely to be applicable to your organization.

1. The trouble with American leaders is their lack of self-knowledge.

2. The trouble with American leaders is their lack of appreciation for the nature of leadership itself.

3. The trouble with American leaders is their focus on concepts that separate (communities, nations, disciplines, fields, methods, etc.), rather than concepts that express our interconnectedness.

4. The trouble with American leaders is their ignorance of the world and of U.S. interdependence—their lack of worldmindedness.

5. The trouble with American leaders is their inattention to values—forgetting to ask "Why?" and "What for?"

6. The trouble with American leaders is that they do not know how to make changes, to analyze "social architecture" [Warren Bennis' term], and to create a team to make something different happen.

7. The trouble with American leaders is an insufficient appreciation of the relevance of stakeholders; of the implications of pluralism; and of the fact that nobody is in charge, and therefore each leader is partly in charge of the situation as a whole.

8. The trouble with American leaders is that they are not sufficiently aware of the context, or the external environment, of whatever it is they are responsible for doing.

Option 9 – An Annual Assessment Instrument

We have always had great respect for Jan Masaoka at CompassPoint and all the good people at BoardSource. As a collaborative effort they produced this detailed and comprehensive assessment tool, which they refer to as a first draft to be adapted for your purposes. We think it is an excellent first draft and may very well suit you if you wish to utilize a more formal and comprehensive assessment instrument with your executive.

Please rate your assessment of each category of performance as Remarkable, Satisfactory, Unsatisfactory or Unknown

Agency-Wide: Program Development and Delivery (Circle one)

a. Ensures that the agency has a long-range strategy which achieves its mission, and toward which it makes consistent and timely progress — R S U Unk

b. Provides leadership in developing program and organizational plans with the board of directors and staff — R S U Unk

c. Meets or exceeds program goals in quantity and quality — R S U Unk

d. Evaluates how well goals and objectives have been met — R S U Unk

e. Demonstrates quality of analysis and judgment in program planning, implementation, and evaluation — R S U Unk

f. Shows creativity and initiative in creating new programs — R S U Unk

g. Maintains and utilizes a working knowledge of significant developments and trends in the field (such as AIDS, developmental disabilities, sustainable agriculture, etc.) — R S U Unk

Comments:

_____

_____

_____

Administration and Human Resource Management (Circle one)

a. Divides and assigns work effectively, delegating appropriate levels of freedom and authority — R S U Unk

b. Establishes and makes use of an effective management team — R S U Unk

c. Maintains appropriate balance between administration and programs — R S U Unk

d. Ensures that job descriptions are developed, and that regular performance evaluations are held and documented — R S U Unk

e. Ensures compliance with personnel policies and state and federal regulations on workplaces and employment — R S U Unk

f. Ensures that employees are licensed and credentialed as required,   R   S   U   Unk
    and that appropriate background checks are conducted.

g. Recruits and retains a diverse staff

h. Ensures that policies and procedures are in place to maximize   R   S   U   Unk
    volunteer involvement

i. Encourages staff development and education, and assists program   R   S   U   Unk
    staff in relating their specialized work to the total program of
    the organization

j. Maintains a climate which attracts, keeps, and motivates a diverse   R   S   U   Unk
    staff of top quality people

Comments:

_____

_____

_____

Community Relations   (Circle one)

a. Serves as an effective spokesperson for the agency; represents the   R   S   U   Unk
    programs and point of view of the organization to agencies,
    organizations, and the general public

b. Establishes sound working relationships and cooperative   R   S   U   Unk
    arrangements with community groups and organizations

Comments:

_____

_____

_____

Financial Management and Legal Compliance   (Circle one)

a. Assures adequate control and accounting of all funds, including   R   S   U   Unk
    developing and maintaining sound financial practices

b. Works with the staff, finance committee, and board in   R   S   U   Unk
    preparing a budget; sees that the organization operates within
    budget guidelines

c. Maintains official records and documents, and ensures compliance   R   S   U   Unk
    with federal, state and local regulations and reporting requirements
    (such as annual information returns, payroll withholding and
    reporting, etc.)

d. Executes legal documents appropriately   R S U Unk

e. Assures that funds are disbursed in accordance with contract R S U Unk
requirements and donor designations

Comments:

_____

_____

_____

Fundraising   (Circle one)

a. Develops realistic, ambitious fundraising plans   R S U Unk

b. Meets or exceeds revenue goals, ensuring that adequate funds R S U Unk
are available to permit the organization to carry out its work

c. Successfully involves others in fundraising   R S U Unk

d. Establishes positive relationships with government, foundation R S U Unk
and corporate funders

e. Establishes positive relationships with individual donors R S U Unk

Comments:

_____

_____

_____

Board of Directors

a. Works well with board officers   R S U Unk

b. Provides appropriate, adequate, and timely information to R S U Unk
the board

c. Provides support to board committees   R S U Unk

d. Sees that the board is kept informed on the condition of the R S U Unk
organization and all important factors influencing it

e. Works effectively with the board as a whole   R S U Unk

Comments:

_____

_____

_____

Option 10 – Core Components for Success

This lends itself to high board participation because it is visually appealing and on one page. We also like the relatively large space for comments, which increases the chance that this will not be a "check the grade and turn it in" process but one that moves toward thoughtful consideration. The executive and the relevant board members each fill in the form independently. All results are given to the board president, who renders them into a single document. The executive committee and executive can then review the results and use them to structure a scheduled, lengthy conversation.

You will have to decide whether these nine abilities are the ones you would pick and whether the evaluators should be anonymous. On the latter, we would tend to vote no, instead encouraging all to be as open as possible with their feedback.

Core Components for Success

The following is the scale to be used:

5 = Excellent   4 = Commendable   3 = Satisfactory

2 = Needs Improvement   1 = Unacceptable   DK = Don't know, no opportunity to observe

Ability	Evaluation						Comment
Conceptual Clarity/Positioning: ability to envision, articulate and place in context an idea/project	☐ 5	☐ 4	☐ 3	☐ 2	☐ 1	☐ DK	
The Product: ability to ensure its quality, its quantitative success	☐ 5	☐ 4	☐ 3	☐ 2	☐ 1	☐ DK	
Participation: ability to assist board and committee members to be significantly involved	☐ 5	☐ 4	☐ 3	☐ 2	☐ 1	☐ DK	
The Plan: ability to devise a comprehensive and feasible strategy involving appropriate board, staff and committee people	☐ 5	☐ 4	☐ 3	☐ 2	☐ 1	☐ DK	
Timeliness: ability to maintain a schedule in the execution of a plan and its final result	☐ 5	☐ 4	☐ 3	☐ 2	☐ 1	☐ DK	
Problem Management: ability to take personal responsibility, proceed positively, seek help as needed, anticipate the problems	☐ 5	☐ 4	☐ 3	☐ 2	☐ 1	☐ DK	
Linking/Connecting: ability to see and make beneficial project/people connections within and to form mutually beneficially linkages without	☐ 5	☐ 4	☐ 3	☐ 2	☐ 1	☐ DK	
Cost Control: ability to work within a budget, accommodate budgetary adjustments efficiently	☐ 5	☐ 4	☐ 3	☐ 2	☐ 1	☐ DK	
Revenue Generation: ability to identify appropriate revenue sources, develop diversity of revenue sources, establish multi-year funding sources, balance earned and unearned income	☐ 5	☐ 4	☐ 3	☐ 2	☐ 1	☐ DK	

Option 11 – Key Relationships for Review and Development

Clearly one of the most important tasks of the not-for-profit executive is to initiate and sustain healthy and mutually beneficial relationships with key constituents. We say "key" and have selected eight. In fact, there may be twice that many or more, but these do seem to rise to the top as most crucial for the leadership of an organization. Rather than a broad, subjective conversation about the nature of the relationships, we propose three questions about each one: How's it going? How can we do better? What are the factors that can strengthen or subvert?

Implied in this series of questions is something beyond the individual executive. There is an aspect of "wellness" involved as in all relationships. Further, we take it to be a board responsibility to assist where appropriate in strengthening the productivity and satisfaction of those relationships key to the life of the organization. We have tried this in chart form, though you may use it otherwise as long as it moves toward a useful conversation.

The Relationship	How's it going?	How can we do better?	Factors that strengthen or subvert?
The Board			
Board President			
Executive Committee			
Committee Chairs			
Staff			
Constituents			
Major Funders			
Colleague Institutions			
The Media			

Option 12 – Contracting for Effectiveness

This format for executive evaluation uses a small number of categories and three to six check-in periods yearly. It focuses on things you want to make happen, with the objective of setting goals that ninety percent of the time will produce a success. This "stacking the deck" on the side of achievement is a direct steal from Tom Peters *(Thriving on Chaos)*, who consistently stresses an appraisal system that emphasizes degrees of winning rather than determining winners and losers. He states, "There is an attribute of goal-setting that stands out in creating a highly charged environment—teaching people that they are winners and that they can succeed, which, in turn, induces them to take on more [and] risk more."

This preamble and expert testimony are meant to entice you into trying an approach that goes against our tendency to inflict unattainable "stretch goals" and our parallel tendency to believe that responding to success and achievement with praise only leads to something between laurel-resting and laziness. Maybe not...

The scheme is that every two to four months the executive meets with the board chair, the head of the personnel committee or someone else they designate. Together, they produce a brief, one-page document listing no more than four items to be agreed upon by both.

The four might include any of the following:

1. Professional growth or career development goals (for example, achieve a specialization in marketing)

2. Skill development goals (for example, learn new database software)

3. Goals related to this year's organizational mission emphasis (for example, develop abilities in media relations)

4. Goals directly connected to relationships or communication within the organization (for example, meet separately with each board member once during the year)

5. Goals related to strategies, processes or structure (for example, develop new personnel manual)

For this experience to work well, there should be no more than four goals for each time period. There is no numerical rating; instead, ample time is allowed for a conversation within the month following the agreed-upon number of weeks or months. This requires fairly major commitment on behalf of all parties. It also will likely produce fairly major results.

Option 13 – Assessing Personal Satisfaction

This evaluation proceeds from the not-too-radical assumption that your organization, in some form or another, is in the life satisfaction business. You want to make people's lives more enriched (arts and culture), more enlightened (education), healthier (health and mental health), more in control (community organization). To be more enriched, healthy, enlightened, and in control is to have a more satisfying life.

The next assumption (also less than radical) is that your organization, while in business to produce satisfaction for people called students, clients, audiences or patients, ought to do so in a way that does not bring dissatisfaction to the lives of your own board, administration and staff. If they get unhealthy, out of control, or lacking in satisfaction, it will be hard to promote your particular brand of life satisfaction successfully to others.

If you are to approach your community with medium and message well in line, the final evaluation of your organization must address the positive impact it has on the lives of all those who come in contact with it. Some of those are called executives and others, board members.

So what will you inquire in this form of evaluation? Here are some ideas to provoke a thoughtful, personal assessment conversation with your executive.

1. What is this organization's impact on the rest of your life?

2. What happens in this organization that makes you proud?

3. What about the organization do you find yourself talking about with anything ranging from satisfaction to glee?

4. How would your life be different if you were not a part of this organization?

5. What do others conclude about the organization by the way you act and speak about it?

6. What specifically would you change to make your experience in the organization more satisfying?

A personally healthy and satisfied executive may be one of the better testimonies to the real effectiveness of your organization in making a positive impact on the community.

Option 14 – Analysis of Pressing Issues

This is an excellent tool with which to engage the whole board. While all organizations have multiple issues, some are clearly urgent priorities. This experience will assist the board and the executive to reach some agreement on just what those are. The focus and energy created by such a conversation in and of itself will begin the forward momentum on those most-urgent matters. We suggest getting started by setting aside 30–45 minutes of a board meeting to do the following:

1. Ask everyone to write down what they believe to be the three or four most urgent priorities facing the organization in the next six months.

2. Prompt them to think of three or four more by saying:

   "Think about internal and external issues."

   "Think also of systems issues and people issues."

   "Think of issues related to our product and those related to our processes."

   "Think of issues carried forward from the past and those beginning to emerge in the future."

3. Collect and combine the issues into one list.

4. Present the combined issues for further discussion about their level of urgency.

5. Select a workable number to focus on for the next six months.

6. Indicate what a reasonable expectation would be for each issue in that time period.

Option 15 – Conversations About Leadership: Inspired by Philosophers and Social Scientists

The use of literary quotes and statements by leadership gurus as ways into important executive-board conversation engendered such positive response from our editorial advisory committee that we have added one final one based on quotations from the writings of philosophers and social scientists.

Examples such as Freud's "In small matters trust the mind, in large ones the heart" open up a great deal about how we make decisions in our organizations. Once again, many of the most important leadership qualities are reflected in these quotes. Utilize them as a creative, indirect way of approaching those issues.

1. "To allow oneself to be carried away by a multitude of conflicting concerns, to surrender to too many demands, to commit oneself to too many projects, to want to help everyone in everything is to succumb to violence." —Thomas Merton

2. "Expediency asks the question: 'Is it political?' Cowardice asks the question: 'Is it safe?' Vanity asks the question: 'Is it popular?' But conscience asks the question: 'Is it right?' " —Martin Luther King, Jr.

3. "Never look down to test the ground before taking your next step; only a person who keeps an eye fixed on the far horizon will find the right road." —Dag Hammerskold

4. "I'm uncomfortable with the notion of adulthood being founded on a static, laminated sense of self...What if we saw a kind of refashioning as one of the tasks of our lives?" —Henry Louis Gates

5. "In small matters trust the mind, in large ones the heart." —Sigmund Freud

6. "It is serious playfulness, this combination of concern and humility that makes it possible to be engaged and carefree at the same time." —Mihaly Csikszentuihalyi

7. "Do you wish people to think well of you? If you do then don't speak well of yourself." —Pascal

8. "It is the dull man who is always sure and the sure man who is always dull." —H.L. Menken

9. "The folly of mistaking a paradox for a discovery, a metaphor for a proof, a torrent of verbiage for a spring of capital truths, and oneself as an oracle is inborn in us." —Paul Valery

10. "Wisdom is the reward you get for a lifetime of listening when you had rather been talking." —Aristotle

Chapter 8

Additional Uses, Additional Reading

When our editorial advisory committee first met to discuss the content of this small book, one of the liveliest of several lively conversations was whether or not to include board evaluation on these pages. After all, if the executive must sit still for evaluation, should not the other major locus for organizational leadership do so as well? Or, to put it as we would rather, if the executive is given the gift of time and effort to pay attention to his or her growth and well-being, should not the board whose growth and well-being we care equally about be given the same gift?

The answer we came up with was "yes, but not in this book." However, as noted by more than one person on the editorial board, some of the processes and inventories included here could also be utilized equally usefully in board evaluation. We imagine the following might most easily translate to use by the board as it reviews its own leadership roles:

#3   **Exemplary Leadership Practices**

#6   **Conversations About Leadership: Inspired by Literature**

#7   **Conversations About Leadership: Inspired by Gurus**

#11   **Key Relationships for Review and Development**

#12   **Contracting for Effectiveness**

#13   **Assessing Personal Satisfaction**

#14   **Analysis of Pressing Issues**

Many of the other approaches could also be useful with very little amendment.

Second, in the executive search process, search committees are always looking for ways to ask good questions and make smart lists to see if candidate John or Jane Doe is a good match for their organization. It seems to us that a few of the inventories and processes herein also lend themselves to use in that very important activity of selecting a new executive. For this we suggest you look at the following, which would require little if any amendment:

#1	**Leadership Roles and Competencies**
#3	**Exemplary Leadership Practices**
#4	**Inventory of Leadership Attributes and Abilities**
#8	**"The Trouble with Leaders" Inventory**
#9	**An Annual Assessment Instrument**
#10	**Core Competencies for Success**

Again, you may note others that would only necessitate minor adjustments in language and format to serve in the process of search and selection.

Finally, if you are wise enough as a board to think about succession planning, many of this book's inventories would be useful. The question of what kind of leadership is needed next and what precise abilities and attributes your organization will need can be addressed via many of the fifteen options described.

Additional Reading

Boyett, Joseph, and Jimmie Boyett. *The Guru Guide: The Best Ideas of the Top Management Thinkers.* New York: Wiley, 1998.

Bennis, Warren. *On Becoming a Leader.* Cambridge: Perseus Books, 1989.

Burns, James MacGregor. *Transforming Leadership.* New York: Atlantic Monthly Press, 2003.

Block, Peter. *Stewardship: Choosing Service Over Self Interest.* San Francisco: Berrett-Koehler Publishers, Inc., 1993.

Carver, John. *Carver Guide 7: Board Assessment of the CEO.* San Francisco: Jossey-Bass, 1997.

Coens, Peter, and Mary Jenkins. *Abolishing Performance Appraisals: Why They Backfire and What to Do Instead.* San Francisco: Berrett-Koehler Publishers, Inc., 2000.

Collins, Jim. *Good to Great and the Social Sector.* Boulder: Collins, 2005.

Drucker, Peter. *The Essential Drucker: The Best of Sixty Years of Peter Drucker's Essential Writings on Management.* New York: HarperCollins Publishers, 2003.

Gardener, John W. *Living, Leading & the American Dream.* San Francisco: Jossey-Bass, 2003.

Greenleaf, Robert K. *Servant Leadership: A Journey into the Nature of Legitimate Power & Greatness (25th anniv. ed.).* New Jersey: Paulist Press, 1977.

Jaworski, Joseph. *Synchronicity: The Inner Path of Leadership.* San Francisco: Berrett-Koehler Publishers, Inc., 1998.

Kohn, Alfie. *Punished by Rewards: The Trouble with Gold Stars, Incentive Plans, A's, Praise, & Other Bribes.* New York: Houghton Mifflin Co., 1993.

Kouzes, James M., and Barry Z. Posner. *Leadership Challenge: The Five Practices of Exemplary Leadership.* San Francisco: Jossey-Bass, 2002.

MacGregor, Douglas. *The Human Side of Enterprise.* Columbus: McGraw-Hill, 2005.

Mintz, Joshua, and Jan Pierson. *Assessment of the Chief Executive: A Tool for Nonprofit Boards (rev. ed.).* Washington, D.C.: BoardSource, 2005.

Palmer, Parker. *A Hidden Wholeness: The Journey Toward an Undivided Life.* San Francisco: Jossey-Bass, 2004.

Peters, Tom. *Thriving on Chaos.* New York: Alfred A. Knopf, Inc., 1987.

Quinn, Robert. *Deep Change: Discovering the Leader Within.* San Francisco: Jossey-Bass, 1996.

Scholtes, Peter. *The Leader's Handbook: Making Things Happen, Getting Things Done.* Columbus: McGraw-Hill, 1998. (Note Chapter 9, "Performance without Appraisal.")

Seijts, Gerard H., and Gary P. Latham. "Learning vs. Performance Goals: When Should Each Be Used?" *Academy of Management Executives.* 19.1 (2005): pp. 124-31.

York, Peter. "Learning As We Go, Making Evaluation Work for Everyone." 2003. The Conservative Company. 7 April 2006. <http://www.tccgrp.com/pdfs/per_brief_lawg.pdf>.

Afterwords

To engage in an evaluative process that invites dialogue and exchange is to give your executive leader gifts of knowledge, understanding and growth. Both your director and your organization will be enriched.
— Barbara Acton, Executive Director

❧

All good leaders direct their own evolution—constantly growing to best serve their changing organization and to sustain themselves. Executive evaluation, carefully considered and thoughtfully done, is a superb way for board members to support their leader's work and growth. The processes and inventories in this book turn the usual, often haphazard approach to executive evaluation on its head. They show us how to take the task from a "have to" to a "get to." It is a superb roadmap to embracing and shaping this crucial process.
— Jan Allen, Board President

❧

Executive evaluation should provide space for reflection on the road traveled to date and the journey ahead. A collaborative effort between the organization and the executive requires time for thoughtful conversations throughout the evaluation process.
— Jeff Biehl, Executive Director

❧

In not-for-profits there is no greater challenge than finding the time to reflect and evaluate. There is also no greater reward. Taking that time allows us to be sure we are staying on mission and continuing to grow personally and professionally.
— Lisa Chambers, Executive Director

❧

Executive evaluations may seem painful to both parties. I tend to think of them as a gift—a gift for the organization's renewal and the recipient's understanding of how the board can support their mutual mission.
— Luke Feck, Board President

❦

With the growing number of organizations led by people of color, a publication like this is culturally relevant, transferable and can be integrated into diversity-rich organizations.
— Ruben Castilla Herrera, Not-for-Profit Manager

❦

It's no secret that the success of an organization and its leader can be enhanced with the exchange of thoughtful and candid communication. Executive evaluation is a genuine opportunity for a board and leader to reflect together, share ideas and clarify expectations. It's a chance to inspire, challenge and motivate each other to advance the mission of the organization.
— Cindy Hilsheimer, Board President

❦

What is left unsaid so often matters the most. The concepts and tools within these covers create a path to rich discussion between executive and board. It creates opportunities to enhance effective leadership and further the organization's mission.
— Eric Ireland, Board President

❦

This book can help boards and executives of not-for-profits seeking a better way to conduct executive evaluation. So many people are affected by the work of not-for-profits that we owe it to our community to do this task well. In the immortal words of Thomas Alva Edison, "If there's a way to do it better...find it."
— Aaron M. Riley, Executive Director

❦

"Just Do It." Yes, this is stolen from the Nike campaign; however, it sums up the point of this book. There are many different ways to conduct an evaluation, and hopefully one of the suggested formats will work for you. The most important thing is putting the evaluation tool to use and conducting a thoughtful, interesting evaluation that helps move your ED and organization forward.
— Janelle Simmons, Not-for-Profit Manager